INVESTIGATING THE UNKNOWN

Amazing
OUT-OF-BODY
Experiences

Carl R. Green and William R. Sanford

E | **Enslow Publishers, Inc.**
40 Industrial Road
Box 398
Berkeley Heights, NJ 07922
USA

http://www.enslow.com

Original edition published as *Out-of-Body Experiences* in 1993.

Library of Congress Cataloging-in-Publication Data

Green, Carl R.
    Amazing out-of-body experiences / Carl R. Green and William R. Sanford ; illustrated by Gerald Kelley.
        p. cm. — (Investigating the unknown)
    Rev. ed. of: Out-of-body experiences.
    Summary: "Explores out-of-body (OBE) and near-death experiences (NDE), including several reported examples of OBEs, the history of OBEs, and research and experiments with OBEs"—Provided by publisher.
    Includes bibliographical references (p.   ) and index.
    ISBN 978-0-7660-3822-6
    1. Astral projection—Juvenile literature. 2. Near-death experiences—Juvenile literature. I. Sanford, William R. (William Reynolds), 1927– II. Kelley, Gerald. III. Green, Carl R. Out-of-body experiences. IV. Title.
    BF1389.A7G72 2012
    133.9'5—dc22   2010044119

Paperback ISBN 978-1-59845-307-2

Printed in China

052011 Leo Paper Group, Heshan City, Guangdong, China

10 9 8 7 6 5 4 3 2 1

To Our Readers: We have done our best to make sure all Internet addresses in this book were active and appropriate when we went to press. However, the author and the publisher have no control over and assume no liability for the material available on those Internet sites or on other Web sites they may link to. Any comments or suggestions can be sent by e-mail to comments@enslow.com or to the address on the back cover.

Illustration Credits: © The Art Gallery Collection / Alamy, p. 27; Associated Press, p. 36; Ernest Hemingway Photograph Collection, John F. Kennedy Presidential Library and Museum, Boston, p. 19 (bottom right); Library of Congress Prints & Photographs, pp. 15, 19 (top left, top right, and bottom left), 21; Mary Evans Picture Library / Everett Collection, p. 22; Courtesy Monroe Institute, p. 32; © Peter Arnold, Inc. / Alamy, p. 38; Réunion des Musées Nationaux / Art Resource, NY, p. 13; Shutterstock.com, pp. 1, 4, 6, 29, 41, 42.

Original Illustrations: © 2010 Gerald Kelley, www.geraldkelley.com, pp. 10, 14, 20, 25, 28, 33, 35, 40.

Cover Illustration: Shutterstock.com (Illustration of person walking toward the light from a dark tunnel).

Contents

Authors' Note

Thanks to science, many of nature's great mysteries have been solved. Do you want to know about earthquakes or earthworms? There's probably an expert somewhere who can answer most of your questions. But wouldn't this be a boring world if we knew all there is to know? Perhaps that's why people want to believe that the mind does possess mysterious powers.

In this series, you'll learn about these mysteries of the unknown:

- *The Mystery of Fortune-Telling*
- *Astonishing Mind Powers*
- *The Mysterious Secrets of Dreams*
- *Amazing Out-of-Body Experiences*
- *Discovering Past Lives*
- *Sensing the Unknown*

Do such mysteries truly exist? Some people say yes, others say no. Once you've studied both sides of the debate, you can decide for yourself. Along the way, keep one important thought in mind. In this field, it is often hard to separate the real from the fake. It pays to be skeptical when setting out to explore the mysteries of the unknown.

A Stranger in the Captain's Cabin

CHAPTER ONE

In 1828, first mate Robert Bruce's ship was six weeks out of Liverpool, England, sailing westward. He thought he knew everyone on board. So who—or what—was this apparition in the captain's cabin? The strange man was calmly writing on a slate. Shaken by the sight, Bruce hurried to tell the captain.

The captain rushed to his cabin. He found the slate, but the stranger was gone. Chalked on it were four words: *Steer to the Nor'west.*

Bruce swore he had not written the message. To prove it, he wrote the same words. His handwriting did not match. The puzzled captain tested his crew with the same results. Was there a stowaway on board? A search of the ship proved fruitless.

The captain studied the message. With the wind at his back, a course change would cost him little. He gave the order to steer to the northwest. Three hours later, a lookout spotted a ship wrecked on an iceberg. Quickly, the ship's boats rescued the stranded crew. Bruce watched as the survivors climbed aboard. One man caught his eye. He felt sure it was the stranger he had seen in the captain's cabin!

At the captain's request, the man wrote *Steer to the Nor'west* on the slate. Bruce's mouth fell open when the captain turned the slate over. The writing on both sides looked the same. "I only wrote one of these," the man said. "Who wrote the other?"

Useful Definitions

Researchers who study the mind have worked hard to define terms used to discuss out-of-body experiences (OBEs). Here are a few of the key words:

astral travel—An older name for an OBE, still favored by psychics. During astral travel, the "astral body" is said to journey outside the physical body. Some psychics claim they can go astral traveling any time they wish.

aura—An ever-changing energy field that psychics say surrounds a living plant, an animal, or a person. Psychics claim they can diagnose illness by the shape and color of a person's aura.

body double—The spirit body that leaves the real body during an OBE. Body doubles are also called astral bodies or doppelgängers.

extrasensory perception (ESP)—The ability to send or receive data without using the normal senses. ESP powers include clairvoyance, telepathy, and precognition.

near-death experience (NDE)—The feeling of having died and left one's body, only to return to take up one's life again.

out-of-body experience (OBE)—The feeling of leaving one's body to travel near and far. During OBEs, people claim to travel as invisible energy bodies or as body doubles. These body doubles pass freely through walls and fly through space.

The tale the man told was simple enough. He had fallen asleep on his stranded ship a few hours earlier. When he woke, he told his shipmates that help was on its way. He even described the rescue ship in exact detail.[1]

This story relates to an age-old mystery—the out-of-body experience, or OBE. The shipwrecked man seemingly left his body and traveled to the nearest ship. There, his body double had chalked a message that led to his rescue. Why didn't he speak to Bruce? No one knows. OBEs do not obey the rules that govern daily life.

Near-death experiences (NDEs) are close cousins of the OBE. In a typical NDE, the Reverend J. L. Bertrand died . . . and then returned to life. Bertrand's NDE took place back in the 1800s. He was climbing in the Swiss Alps. Feeling weary, he told the guide to take the other people in his group on to the top. As he lay in the snow, he found he could no longer move his arms and legs. His head ached with the cold. A thought popped into his mind: *I am freezing to death!*

All at once, Bertrand felt himself leave his body. Looking down, he saw himself lying in the snow. He felt as though he were floating, held to that distant body by a thin cord. Soon, he was high enough to see his fellow climbers. As he watched them, the guide sneaked a chicken leg from the lunch pack. Bertrand felt very sad that the cord still tied him to his old life.

Moments later he saw the returning climbers find his body. The guide rubbed Bertrand's pale face and arms, trying to start the blood flowing again. Bertrand felt himself being pulled downward. With a silent scream, he passed back into his body. In that instant, he knew he was alive once more. He sat up suddenly and scolded the startled guide for stealing the chicken leg.[2]

History is full of stories of OBEs and NDEs. Perhaps one day we will solve the puzzle of what they mean and how they happen. For now, we can only say that the mind hides its secrets all too well.

The Reverend J. L. Bertrand looks down on his body, which he left lying in the snow during a near-death experience. As his NDE progressed, he felt sad to find that he was still tied to his earth-bound body.

AMAZING OUT-OF-BODY EXPERIENCES

CHAPTER TWO

OBEs Past and Present

Olga Worrall, alone and afraid, went to sleep with her bedroom light on. About an hour later, the British housewife awoke to see her husband standing by her bed. Although she knew he was away on a trip, she did not feel frightened.

"Put out the lights!" he seemed to say. Olga did as she was told. Then she went back to sleep.

When Worrall returned a few days later, he described what he thought was a dream. In the dream, he said, he walked through the house. As he neared the bedroom, he saw that the light was on. Reaching out to switch it off, his hand went through the wall. That was when he told Olga to turn the light out. As soon as she obeyed, Worrall woke up—in his hotel bed.[1]

Were husband and wife sharing the same dream? After all, dreams take up two or more hours of each night's sleep. But research shows that dreams grow out of your own store of memories. No one else shares your dreams. Scientists who study reports of OBEs can only shake their heads. No hard evidence of the existence of astral bodies has been found. What people call OBEs, they say, may result from dream activity or an ESP event.

Whatever their origin, OBEs are far from dreamlike. Those who claim to have had an OBE return with vivid reports of their travels. In a typical OBE, a body double leaves the sleeping body and floats above it. Sometimes the body on the bed seems to shudder and become stiff. The double appears to be attached to the body, often by a thin, silver cord. The astral body feels weightless and more alive than ever. The senses seem sharper, colors seem brighter.

Free to travel, the astral body walks through walls or soars high into the sky. During these journeys, the cord stretches but does not break. OBEs end when the body double returns to the physical body. Often it slips back in without effort. At other times, it enters with a jerk that wakes the sleeper. Either way, people who return from OBEs feel a sense of inner peace. Thoughts of death no longer fill them with fear.

No one knows when the first OBE took place. In early cultures, priests often put themselves into trances. The trance, they said, allowed their souls to find and speak to the gods. In ancient Egypt, OBEs were part of religious beliefs. Each person was said to possess a *ka* and a *ba*. The ka was a body double that lived on in the tomb after death. That freed the ba to travel on to the next world. In modern India, yogis enter trance states in which they claim to leave their bodies.

Over 2,500 years ago, the king of Syria led an army into Israel. Each time the Syrians attacked, the Israelite army was waiting. "Who is giving

Ancient Egyptian artwork depicts the ba, the bird-soul, hovering above a corpse. The Egyptians believed that the ba traveled on to the next world, while the body double (the ka) stayed in the tomb.

away our plans?" the king roared. A member of the court told him about a prophet named Elisha. This Israelite, the man said, knows everything that is said in your tent. Perhaps the king believed that Elisha was using his astral body to visit his tent. Certain that he had found the spy, he laid siege to the prophet's city.

Once again the king of Syria ran into powers far beyond his own. Elisha asked God to blind his foes. Then Elisha led the army of blind men into the Israelite camp. When their sight was restored the Syrians saw they were captives. They laid down their arms and marched home.[2]

Did the biblical prophet Elisha travel out of body to spy on the Syrians? Whether Elisha did or not, the Syrian king acted as if he believed it.

Even the great Greek thinkers of ancient times believed in OBEs. Plato was certain that the soul could leave the body and travel freely. Plotinus wrote of "being lifted out of the body into myself."[3]

The writer Hermotimus often seemed to wander far from his stiff, still body. "Do not touch me while I am gone," he told his wife. But the wife, upset by her husband's apparent absences, wanted to teach him a lesson. During one of his OBEs, she asked two friends to move his body. Sadly, the two men turned out to be rivals, not friends. They declared that Hermotimus was dead. Then they burned the body.[4]

Lucky Lindy's OBE

After World War I, brave pilots competed to set records for speed and distance. In 1927, Charles Lindbergh joined the ranks of aviation's greatest heroes. "Lucky Lindy" captured the nation's heart by flying nonstop from New York to Paris.

Once he was airborne, Lindbergh faced a flight of more than thirty hours. Twenty-two hours after takeoff, the *Spirit of St. Louis* flew into a thick fog. As the plane droned on through the gray mist, Lindbergh fought to stay awake. Then, he revealed years later, he seemed to slip into an OBE.

Lindbergh wrote that he seemed to exist outside of "time and matter." He felt himself "departing from my body as I imagine a spirit would depart." Drifting upward and outward, he seemed to pass through the frame of the plane. Then he floated in midair, "far distant from the human form I left [behind]." All this time, he was bound to his body by a long cord. The cord was so thin, he wrote, "it could have been snapped by a breath."

Lindbergh knew that his "vision" could have been caused by fatigue. That kind of logic made sense—but the pilot set logic aside. He knew what he had seen and felt. The longer he lived, he wrote in his autobiography, the more he doubted that science has all the answers.[5]

Charles Lindbergh claimed to have an OBE during his transatlantic flight in the *Spirit of St. Louis*. Was it fatigue, or did "Lucky Lindy" truly depart from his body?

When researchers study OBEs, some basic facts emerge.

- ✦ The world has changed but accounts of OBEs stay constant. An OBE described by a Texas cowboy closely resembles those reported by ancient Greeks.

- ✦ Most people report only one OBE in a lifetime. Their OBEs often take place during stressful events such as an illness or car crash.

- ✦ No one who has had an OBE ever forgets it. Many people see their OBEs as proof that they will live on after death.

- ✦ OBEs are nearly always pleasant. But once the astral travel ends, most people refuse to talk about their journeys. They worry that their friends will think they have lost their minds.

- ✦ During an OBE people often "see" events they could not have seen with their normal senses. Experts suggest that the subjects may have used ESP—or they may have been astral traveling.

Scientific studies of OBEs face two problems. First, most people cannot summon an OBE at will. That fact makes it very hard to set up controlled studies in a lab. Second, few astral travelers are trained observers. Most are too involved in their once-in-a-lifetime "trip" to make good mental notes.

Writers seem to have OBEs more often than most people do. Could it be their vibrant imaginations? A number of famous authors have reported out-of-body experiences, including (clockwise from top left) Leo Tolstoy, Jack London, Ernest Hemingway, and Edgar Allan Poe.

British author William Gerhardie claimed that he could go on an **OBE** whenever he wished. He said that during an **OBE**, he was always tied to his body by a glowing silver cord. Most people who report **OBEs** also describe being attached to their bodies by a similar cord.

Gerhardie was not the first to describe a "silver cord" linking astral and physical bodies. The term appears in the Bible. The twelfth chapter of Ecclesiastes says, " . . . the mourners go about the streets . . . before the silver cord is loosed." An American expert, Sylvan Muldoon, has tried to describe the cord. He believes it is one and one-half inches thick at the moment the astral and human bodies divide. As the astral body roams, the cord stretches as thin as a thread. Energy appears to pass through the cord from the astral body to the human body. Some writers report that it is attached to the forehead. Others say it is hooked to the body's navel or the back of the head.[5]

Those who glimpse astral travelers do not always see the thin, silver cord. Mark Twain, author of *Tom Sawyer,* wrote about such an event. Twain happened to see a stranger approach his house one day. As he watched, the man walked to within twenty feet of where he stood. Then, in the blink of an eye, he was gone! Twain, a big fan of psychic events, was delighted. "I had seen a [ghost] at

Author Mark Twain believed he had seen a ghost! But most OBE experts think Twain actually saw a man's body double.

Astral Flyer or Astral Fraud?

Madame Helena Petrovna Blavatsky left Russia for the West in the 1800s. At first, she wandered through Europe, holding séances. Her journeys then led her to New York, where she met Henry Olcott.

In 1875, Blavatsky and Olcott founded a group devoted to the study of what they called theosophy. They took the name for their beliefs from the Greek words for "god" and "wisdom." Followers gathered to learn "the magic of the ancients" from HPB (Helena Blavatsky's initials). Humans, she said, exist on many planes beyond the earthly one. HPB added that she often traveled via her astral body.

Helena Petrovna Blavatsky

Critics attacked her work and revealed past scandals. To escape, HPB moved to India. There, she told the world, she made contact with a race of Masters. Theosophy revived and prospered.

The Society for Psychical Research (SPR) sent Richard Hodgson to check up on her. Hodgson soon decided that the "miracles" were just clever tricks. Although his report charged that HPB was a fraud, her followers ignored it. Their faith was rewarded a hundred years later. In 1986, the SPR agreed that Hodgson had not fully proven his case.[6]

last, with my own eyes," he told himself. But more surprises lay ahead. When Twain entered the house, the stranger was waiting for him. A servant had welcomed the man into the house some time earlier.[7]

OBE experts believe that Twain saw the man's double, not a ghost. The man was already seated inside when his double retraced his steps to the door. Why would a body double repeat such a simple act? No one knows.

Strange as it seems, many people say they have had an OBE. In 1890, a British survey asked 17,000 people if they had been in touch with an astral body. Ten percent answered yes. Of these, one in three claimed to have seen doubles of living people. Almost a century later, a new survey turned up similar numbers. The 1975 study asked a thousand Americans if they had traveled out of body. Fourteen percent of the adults and 25 percent of the students said yes.[8] It appears that OBEs and NDEs are still going strong.

CHAPTER FOUR

Standing at the Edge

Private George Ritchie came down with the flu during World War II. In the army hospital, his fever peaked at 106.5 degrees. That night, as in a dream, he awoke and jumped out of bed. Behind him, he said later, he saw what looked like a dead man wearing his ring. Out in the hall, a nurse walked right through him. In the next instant, he was flying through the night. When he tried to touch a phone line, his hand could not grasp it. Confused by his ghost-like state, he flew back to the hospital.

George flitted from room to room, looking at each sleeping man. At last, he found his own body, covered by a sheet. All at once the room seemed to fill with light. George saw scenes from his life flash by. Then he saw wonderful new worlds beyond earth. "Look at all I have missed," George told himself. Then he slipped back inside his own body.

Seeing signs of life in the "corpse," a doctor injected George with a strong drug. In what the doctor called "a miracle," life surged back.

Although George had been "dead" for nine minutes, his brain was not harmed. After the war, his NDE led him to the task of caring for mental patients. He returned from the dead, he said, to "learn about man and then serve God." He assured patients who came to him with similar tales that they were not insane.[1]

Private George Ritchie looks at his sheet-covered body before reentering it during his World War II NDE.

George Ritchie would enjoy a painting that hangs in Venice, Italy. Hieronymus Bosch painted the *Ascent of the Blessed* more than five centuries ago. The work shows the souls of the dead moving upward through a long tunnel. The tunnel leads to a pure yellow light and a divine being. People who have NDEs believe that death frees the soul to travel toward that healing light.

Kimberly Clark Sharp of Kansas knows about the power of that light. When she was twenty-two, she collapsed on a sidewalk. At first, she said, she found herself lost in a dense, gray fog. Then the fog vanished as the world flooded with light. "It was so bright, the sun is not as bright, yet it didn't hurt my eyes," she remembers. "It filled up everything, and I . . . was back with my Creator." Kimberly felt a sense of love beyond anything she had ever known. "It was heaven, more than ecstasy," she says. "It was a reunion of the highest order."[2]

Most accounts of NDEs repeat these feelings. People are aware of leaving their bodies, often by floating outward. They can hear loved ones crying over their death. Instead of being frightened or in pain, they feel at peace. Many say they hear beautiful music. Long-dead friends appear to assure them that all is well. The world beyond this one, the astral travelers say, is hard to picture. The living cannot imagine a world without limits of time and space.

Many astral travelers say they fly at high speed through a very dark tunnel, cave, or deep well. One person said it was like "I was moving very, very fast in time and space. I was traveling through a tunnel.

People who have experienced an **NDE** feel a kinship with this five-hundred-year-old painting. Hieronymus Bosch called his masterpiece *Ascent of the Blessed*.

Many people who report OBEs and NDEs say they soar through a dark tunnel. In time, the surrounding darkness gives way to a bright light that attracts them toward the end of the tunnel.

It didn't look like a tunnel, but when you're in a tunnel, all you see is blackness around you."[3]

A light appears far ahead of the travelers. As the light grows brighter, they see that it comes from a warm, loving being. Many think of the being as God. A wise voice counsels and teaches them. Sometimes they are allowed to view their lives from birth onward. This life review flashes past like a film run at high speed.

NDEs Lead to a Better Life

Young Stuart Twemlow fell into a washtub. As he floated facedown, he felt relaxed and at peace. His life flashed before him. Instead of gratitude, he felt angry when his mother pulled him out. "I was enjoying where I was," he says. That NDE taught him to treasure each minute. "The NDE has a healing effect," he tells all who will listen.[4]

A young woman confirms Stuart's story. Pat (not her real name) recalls that her life was a mess. She was hooked on drugs and alcohol. Her NDE came during a suicide attempt. The brush with death, she says, taught her that "I'm supposed to be alive."

Pat gave up drugs and turned to helping other addicts. Before the NDE, she adds, "I was into blaming a lot of people. So it's almost like my whole . . . life has changed. . . . I'm reaching out a lot more than I did. I was really self-centered, and I'm growing out of that."[5]

Millions of Americans say they have had an NDE. Few of them, most likely, went looking for their close brush with death. Almost all of them agree on one thing. NDEs changed their lives—for the better.

People who claim to have had an NDE often say their life flashes before their eyes.

A moment later, the NDE reaches a turning point. Death lies on the far side of a fence, a river, or beyond a line of tall trees. If you cross over, the voice says, you cannot come back. Many say they yearn for the peace that awaits "over there." They choose life, they say, because they still have work to do. Making that choice returns them to their bodies.

Many who have NDEs wonder if the experience was real. Hoping to prove that they are sane, they seek out others who have taken the same journey. Accepting the truth of their NDEs changes their lives. Given a new start, they pack each day with joy and good works. Because they no longer fear death, they begin to live life to the fullest. People who had never before experienced deep religious feelings develop a strong new faith.[6]

Do NDEs give us a true picture of what happens when we die? No one knows for sure. After all, we have only the words of those who have escaped almost certain death. For their part, scientists reject events that cannot be tested in a laboratory. For the moment, all we can do is wonder, hoping to learn more.

Science Takes a Look

Robert Monroe is one of the pioneers in OBE exploration. He reports that he first traveled out of body in 1958. Since then, Monroe claims to have had thousands of OBEs. Unlike his fellow travelers, he does not claim that astral journeys prove there is life after death. Take them for what they are, he says.

Monroe says most of his trips were pleasant, a few less so. At times, he met other astral travelers. Some helped him, others attacked him. The attackers, he says, were evil, sub-human beings. As often happens in NDEs, he also met an "energy presence" of great power. Once in a while he found it hard to reenter his body. One scary moment came, he writes, when he slipped into a stranger's dead body by mistake.

To help his search, Monroe set up a lab to study OBEs in a scientific way. In 1975, he took out a patent on a device he calls Hemi-Sync. It is supposed to allow the mind to stay alert while the body falls asleep. In this state, some subjects say they can actually leave their bodies. Like Monroe, they report contact with the spirits of the dead. Some add that

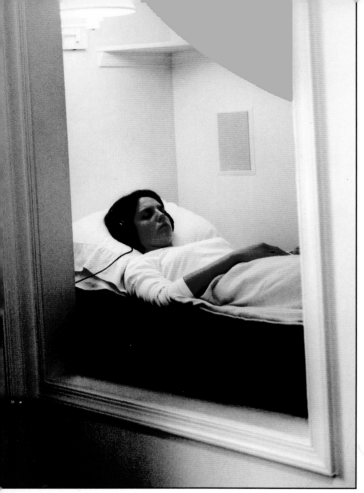

Robert Monroe, a pioneer in the study of OBEs, set up a lab and patented a device called Hemi-Sync that tests for OBEs. This subject is sleeping in a Hemi-Sync booth during one of Monroe's studies.

they reach a state of bliss after meeting with a presence they believe is God.[1]

Science sets high standards in its search for truth. Monroe may be sincere, scientists say, but his work is flawed. Can he be trusted to run tests that might deny his beliefs? The data that Monroe gathers is also suspect. Can his subjects be trusted? In their hypnotic state, they may be telling Monroe what they know he wants to hear.

Even if these doubts were resolved, some questions would remain. Drug users, the mentally ill, and the sick sometimes "see" and "hear" weird sights and sounds. Some drug users, for instance, say they are floating in another world. Many mental hospitals have at least one inmate who claims to be able to "talk" to God. Patients coming out of surgery often hear voices no one else can hear. What about the bright light seen during an NDE? The firing of certain brain cells can create a point of light behind closed eyes. Seeing this bright light can give the patient the illusion of being in a tunnel.

Back in 1966, Dr. Charles Tart of the University of Virginia tried to answer these doubts. His subject, known as Miss Z, said her OBEs had begun when she was a child. As part of the test, Tart placed a five-digit number on a high shelf. At one point during the fourth night of the

Dr. Charles Tart put Miss Z through a test for OBEs. During the test, Miss Z slept while connected to an EEG machine. On the fourth night of the test, Miss Z woke up and called out the five-digit number that Dr. Tart had hidden on a high shelf. How did she do this? Was it an OBE or ESP? It is impossible to know for sure.

test, the sleeping woman's brain waves showed a new pattern. Was this an OBE? When she woke up, Miss Z called off the correct numbers: 2-5-1-3-2. She had beaten odds of 99,999 to 1! Even then, Tart had to admit that the test did not provide final proof. Instead of an OBE, Miss Z might have used ESP to "see" the numbers.[2]

Interest in OBEs kept growing. Dr. Robert Morris of the Psychical Research Foundation in North Carolina tried a new approach. He chose college student Keith Harary as his subject. In one test, Morris put Keith in a closed room. His task was to travel via OBE to a second building. There, he would try to view cutout letters arranged by a technician. After each OBE, he was told to write down what he had seen. At times, Keith beat the odds by scoring a high number of "hits." On other tries he scored poorly. Once he "saw" two people in the room. Morris checked and found that a second man had walked in during the test.[3]

Would cats be aware of an astral body? Keith began a new set of tests by making friends with a kitten named Spirit. Then the kitten was taken to a second room. An observer counted its every move. Researchers ran the test four times, but told Keith to contact the kitten only twice. Each time he did so, Spirit froze in his tracks. His eyes appeared to focus on something the observer could not see. During one non-OBE period, Spirit meowed thirty-seven times. When Keith was "present" during an OBE trial, the kitten did not meow at all.[4]

Do OBEs and NDEs exist? Despite all of the tests and firsthand reports, science is still skeptical. But researchers are not giving up. They are still hoping to find a valid way to explain the how and why of OBEs.

Keith Harary tested his ability to travel out of body with a kitten named Spirit. An observer reported that during Keith's OBEs, the cat appeared to focus on something that no one else could see. Spirit would stop meowing if Keith was "present."

If you wish, you can join in an OBE study. The American Society for Psychical Research (ASPR) in New York City has set up an online questionnaire to collect stories of exceptional experiences and NDEs at <http://www.aspr.com/question.htm>. Anyone who has had an OBE, NDE, or other psychic experience is urged to fill out the questionnaire.

A Film Star Enters a New Age

Actress Shirley MacLaine is one of the millions who says she has traveled out of body. Unlike most of the others, she talks freely about her astral voyages.

MacLaine had her first OBE while she was in Peru in 1975. One night, sitting in a warm bath, she began to stare at a candle flame. All at once, she felt a tunnel open in her mind. "I felt myself become the flame," she writes. "I had no arms, no legs, no body. . . . I felt myself . . . rising out of my body until I began to soar."

MacLaine's astral body flew into space. Below her lay the Andes Mountains. A shining silver cord linked her to her body. As she flew higher, she found she could see the curve of the earth. At that point, she turned back. Gently she flowed back into her body. She felt, she says, like a bit of "Universal Energy."[5]

Actress Shirley MacLaine is a leader in the New Age movement. She has authored many books about the subject. Here she greets her fans at a 2003 book signing.

Thanks to her books and films, MacLaine has become a leader in the New Age movement. New Agers believe in such things as OBEs and past lives. Mental health experts look at these beliefs and hold up a caution sign. Do not, they warn, let New Age psychics make your life choices for you.

Setting Sail on an Astral Voyage

Carol Ann Liaros once worked at the Human Dimensions Institute in Buffalo, New York. There, she tried to teach blind people to "read" colors with their hands. She reports that a few seemed to make progress toward that goal. To her surprise, some of her subjects also learned to "mind travel" via OBEs. While fully relaxed, for instance, they pictured themselves flying to a friend's house. There, they "saw" people and objects.

One woman described details as small as toys scattered on the front porch. A second subject said, "Awareness of my own energy field is developing. . . . I feel as though I can really see myself. . . . I seem to be able to almost see what is in a room. It seems that I really see it, although I don't, and I am totally blind."[1]

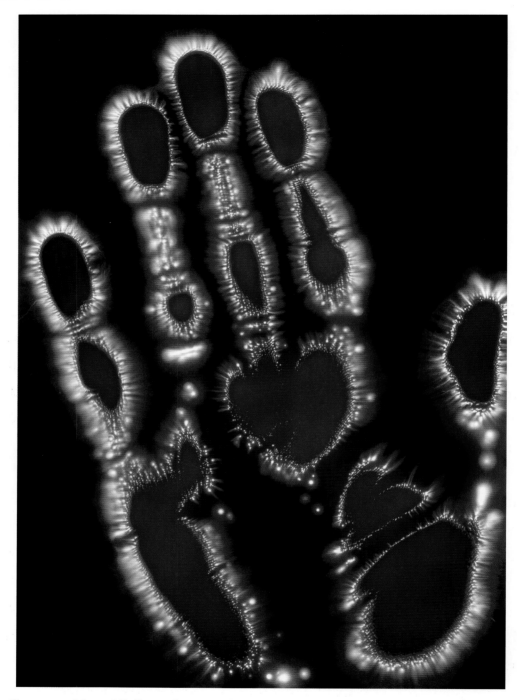

Captured in a Kirlian photo, a human hand reveals the distinctive aura produced by all living things.

Describing the technique of astral travel is simple. Whether the technique will work or not is a much more complex question. Experts in the field say that almost all OBEs are pleasant. Most travelers want to go again and again. Only a handful of people say their OBEs turned into frightening nightmares. These astral travelers tell of feeling pain, pressure, and terror.

Someone who seeks an OBE must be very relaxed. One good way to calm the mind is to meditate. Find a quiet room and lie back against some pillows. With eyes closed, repeat a special sound over and over. Words like "ommmmm" with lots of m's seem to work well. Breathe deeply and clear the mind of all but that special sound. Give the process ten or fifteen minutes. Do not be upset if distracting thoughts creep into your mind. This is normal. Resolve to try again the next day. After all, no one learns to play winning tennis the first day out. Learning to meditate takes practice, too.

Psychics believe that OBEs are related to the body's energy field— its aura. Kirlian photos show that all living things, plant and animal, produce distinctive auras. You may not have to depend on Kirlian photography to see an aura, however. Take a friend (let's call her Nancy) into a dimly lit room. Ask Nancy to stand a foot away from a dark background. Face her from eight to ten feet away. Turn your head and look at her out of the corners of your eyes. With any luck, you will see her aura as a halo of bright light.[2]

Skeptics scoff at tests like this one. Auras, they say, are just clouds of water vapor. Colors appear, they explain, when light is refracted by

Psychics claim they can diagnose an illness based on the color of the patient's aura. Skeptics, however, argue that auras are just clouds of water vapor.

Anyone who seeks an **OBE** is advised to use meditation to calm the mind and body. This young woman is using yoga techniques as a way of gaining the necessary control.

the water droplets. What skeptics cannot explain is the fact that auras appear to vary with the subject's health. Psychics even claim they can diagnose illness by the shape and color of someone's aura.

Those who order themselves to see auras or go out of body are likely to fail. People who fear loss of contact seldom stray far from their bodies during an OBE. Other people worry that they will meet evil spirits. It is

A mandala is a geometric figure that leads the eye back to the center. Because staring at a mandala helps focus the mind and screens out distractions, it is often used as an aid to meditation.

said that most people lose these fears as they glory in their newfound freedom. They often feel themselves soaring skyward, safe from all earthly cares. The goal is to empty the mind and leave it open to the OBE. Some people reach that point fairly quickly. Others take weeks or months to attain their first OBE.

Most of us never reach that point, for reasons no one can clearly explain. Even so, the effort is not wasted. Meditation does a good job of easing the stress of daily living . . . and that's a worthwhile outcome all on its own.

Chapter Notes

Chapter 1. A Stranger in the Captain's Cabin

1. Stuart Holroyd, *Psychic Voyages* (Garden City, N.Y.: Doubleday, 1977), pp. 6–8.

2. Ibid., pp. 86–88.

Chapter 2. OBEs Past and Present

1. Brad Steiger, *Astral Projection* (Rockport, Mass.: Para Research, 1982), pp. 49–50.

2. The Bible, II Kings 6:8–22 (AV).

3. Rosemary Ellen Guiley, *Harper's Encyclopedia of Mystical & Paranormal Experience* (New York: HarperCollins, 1991), p. 420.

4. Herbert B. Greenhouse, *The Astral Journey* (Garden City, N.Y.: Doubleday, 1975), p. 23.

5. Charles A. Lindbergh, *Autobiography of Values* (New York: Harcourt Brace Jovanovich, 1976), pp. 11–12.

Chapter 3. Tied by a Silver Cord

1. Herbert B. Greenhouse, *The Astral Journey* (Garden City, N.Y.: Doubleday, 1975), p. 189.

2. Stuart Holroyd, *Psychic Voyages* (Garden City, N.Y.: Doubleday, 1977), pp. 20–21.

3. Greenhouse, p. 188.

4. Benjamin Walker, *Beyond the Body* (London: Routledge & Kegan Paul, 1974), p. 65.

5. Greenhouse, pp. 46–47.

6. Rosemary Ellen Guiley, *Harper's Encyclopedia of Mystical & Paranormal Experience* (New York: HarperCollins, 1991), pp. 64–66.

7. Greenhouse, pp. 187–188.

8. Guiley, p. 421.

Chapter 4. Standing at the Edge

1. Stuart Holroyd, *Psychic Voyages* (Garden City, N.Y.: Doubleday, 1977), pp. 88–92.

2. Verlyn Klinkenborg, "At the Edge of Eternity," *Life*, March 1992, p. 66.

3. Carol Zaleski, *Otherworld Journeys: Accounts of Near-Death Experience in Medieval and Modern Times* (New York: Oxford University Press, 1987), p. 122.

4. Klinkenborg, p. 71.

5. Zaleski, p. 144.

6. Hans Eysenck and Carl Sargent, *Explaining the Unexplained* (London: Weidenfield & Nicolson, 1982), p. 160.

Chapter 5. Science Takes a Look

1. Rosemary Ellen Guiley, *Harper's Encyclopedia of Mystical & Paranormal Experience* (New York: HarperCollins, 1991), pp. 422–423.

2. Editors of Time-Life, *Psychic Voyages* (Alexandria, Va.: Time-Life, 1987), pp. 35–36.

3. Ibid., p. 41.

4. Richard Broughton, *Parapsychology: The Controversial Science* (New York: Ballantine Books, 1991), pp. 249–251.

5. *Psychic Voyages*, p. 45.

Chapter 6. Setting Sail on an Astral Voyage

1. Herbert B. Greenhouse, *The Astral Journey* (Garden City, N.Y.: Doubleday, 1975), pp. 339–340.

2. William Jon Watkins, *The Psychic Experiment Book* (Englewood Cliffs, N.J.: Prentice-Hall, 1980), pp. 44–45.

Glossary

apparition—An unexpected or unusual sight. Scientists generally prefer to use this term in place of the term "astral body."

astral body—Another name for the body double. During an OBE, the astral body is said to leave the physical body as it begins its journeys.

astral travel—An older name for an OBE. Some psychics claim they can go astral traveling any time they wish.

aura—An ever-changing energy field that psychics say surrounds all living plants, animals, and people.

body double—The nonphysical body that leaves the real body during an OBE. Body doubles are also called astral bodies or doppelgängers.

brain waves—Electric impulses produced by the brain, as measured on an EEG (electroencephalogram) machine.

clairvoyance—The power to perceive events that occur beyond the range of one's normal senses. Some researchers believe that what seem to be OBEs are actually clairvoyant events.

Kirlian photos—Photographs taken of living organisms in the presence of a high-voltage electrical field. Kirlian photos show subjects surrounded by glowing, colored halos of light that are thought to be auras.

meditation—A process that relaxes the body by freeing the mind of all distracting thoughts.

near-death experience (NDE)—The feeling of having died and left one's body, only to return to life some time later.

New Age—A catch-all term for a broad collection of psychic beliefs. While few New Agers would agree on the details, most believe in OBEs, crystal power, ESP, and past lives.

precognition—The power to foretell events before they happen.

prophet—A wise man or woman through whom the will of God (or the gods) is expressed.

psychic—Someone who claims powers that cannot be explained by natural law.

séance—A meeting at which people try to contact the spirits of the dead.

silver cord—The stretchy cord that is said to tie the body double to the physical body during an OBE.

skeptic—Someone who questions widely accepted beliefs or theories.

stowaway—Someone who hides on a ship or plane in order to obtain free passage.

telepathy—Mind-to-mind communication between two or more people.

Further Reading

Books

Austin, Joanne P. *ESP, Psychokinesis, and Psychics*. New York: Chelsea House Publishers, 2008.

Herbst, Judith. *Beyond the Grave*. Minneapolis, Minn.: Lerner Publications Company, 2005.

Jackson, Donna M. *Phenomena: Secrets of the Senses*. New York: Little, Brown and Co., 2008.

McCormick, Lisa Wade. *Near-Death Experiences: The Unsolved Mystery*. Mankato, Minn.: Capstone Press, 2009.

McIntosh, Kenneth and Marsha McIntosh. *The Popularity of Meditation & Spiritual Practices: Seeking Inner Peace*. Philadelphia: Mason Crest Publishers, 2006.

Walker, Kathryn. *Mysteries of the Mind*. New York: Crabtree Pub. Co., 2010.

Internet Addresses

American Society for Psychical Research (ASPR): Exceptional Experiences and Near-Death Experiences Questionnaire
  <http://www.aspr.com/question.htm>

How Stuff Works: How Near-Death Experiences Work
  <http://science.howstuffworks.com/science-vs-myth/extrasensory-perceptions/near-death-experience.htm>

The Skeptic's Dictionary: Out-of-Body Experience (OBE)
  <http://www.skepdic.com/obe.html>

Index